FOXY'S TALE

The True Story of a Champion Alaskan Sled Dog

Library of Congress Catalog Card Number: 94-61595

IBSN 0-9644171-0-3

First Printing - April 1995
Second Printing - March 1996

Cover Design and Illustrations by Charles Lindemuth

Book Design by Carter B. Productions

Whitehouse Publishing
5750 Jordan Circle
Anchorage, Alaska 99504-4363
(907) 333-4105

Printed in Anchorage, Alaska

Dedicated to all the junior dog mushers and puppies that have or will in the future form the special bond that can only exist between a dog and a child on the runners of a sled.

FOXY'S TALE

The True Story of a Champion Alaskan Sled Dog

Ed White and Donna Freedman

Illustrations by
Charles Lindemuth

Whitehouse Publishing   Anchorage, Alaska

ACKNOWLEDGEMENTS

Michael Amaral - We will never be able to thank Michael enough for allowing us to have this extraordinary dog. Foxy has touched our lives in a way that's impossible to explain.

Carter B. - Without this special friend, we would not have been able to share Foxy's story.

Sandy White - She has always been there for Kelly and me, but we have never thanked her enough. This is my feeble attempt to do so.

CHAPTER 1

I n the beginning, there were three sounds.
The best one, the one to which I crept
even before my eyes were open, was the
sound of my mother's heartbeat.

The second was the wild nighttime howl of
the Alaskan wind. Some nights it sounded
very angry. Other nights it sounded like a
wild animal pounding against our house,
trying to knock down the walls.

The third sound, and the most unforgettable,
was the combined voices of the other dogs.
On the stormiest nights, their howls could
barely be heard over the stronger, wilder
voice of the wind. When the nights were
calm, their howls rose in a chorus of ghostly
sounds that made me shiver.

My mother would lie very still in her bed of
straw, curled protectively around her six
puppies. Yet even while she cuddled and
nudged us gently with her cool nose, she was
always half-listening to the howls of the wind
and the other dogs. My brothers and sisters
and I would feel her quivering slightly, as
though she wanted to leave us behind and
take her place among them.

We knew she loved us, but we also knew she wanted to be out on the trail again with Michael, our owner. She was a lead dog on his racing sled dog team. She was smart and very fast.

My mother would tell us about the other dogs in the lot, how fast and strong they were, and how well they worked as a team. "Sled dogs aren't like other dogs;"she said, "we're not pets. We work. We are happiest when we are running in a team and pulling a sled." I listened, but was still too young to understand.

There were 12 other dogs in the dog lot in Michael's backyard. Each dog was tied to a pole in front of a little house. My mother (Michael called her Rosie) had a bigger house surrounded by a fence for her 6 puppies. Michael named me Judy, and called the other puppies Lips, Eveready, Stripes, Jake, and Bouncer.

I liked belonging to Michael. He fed us special meals he cooked over a fire in the yard when the weather was nice, and in a shed

when the weather was stormy. He mixed salmon, beaver, liver and other kinds of meat with chunks of fat to keep us warm during the cold winter nights. He simmered the meal slowly until the rumbling of hungry dog bellies was drowned out by our howls.

Michael always had a few minutes to spend with each of us, calling us by name and roughhousing with us. Sometimes he called me "Squirt," which my mother told me meant that I was little. I was the smallest puppy, but I didn't like that name. My mother kept telling me, "Be patient Judy, you will grow someday."

One day Michael opened the pen and let us out. The snow had melted and green grass was beginning to poke through the mud in the yard. The warm air felt soft and mild, and our winter coats were falling out in clumps.

Michael would play a game with us when he let us out of our pen. He would walk way over to the other side of the yard and then call us to come to him. We would run as fast as we could to get to him. I was always the first puppy to get to Michael. He would pat me on the head and say, "Judy, you sure are fast for a little one."

That's when I started thinking that maybe being little wasn't so bad after all.

One day, Michael didn't let us out to play as he usually did. Instead, he spent the whole morning cleaning up the dog lot. Then he went into his house and got dressed in really fancy clothes, instead of his usual boots and jeans.

Soon cars started pulling into the yard. People walked around, talking and eating things from a table Michael had set up. One of the people, a little one with curly red hair, came over to our pen. She opened the door, but didn't let us out. Instead, she came in and closed the door behind her. No person but Michael had ever been in our pen before, and we didn't know what to do.

She smiled and clapped her hands saying, "Come here, puppies!" My brothers and sisters didn't move. My mother just sat there, watching us. I ran over to the little girl and

jumped up on her. She laughed. Then the rest of the puppies ran over and we all played with her for a long time.

Much later, a man came over to the pen and said, "Come on Kelly, it's time to go." The girl looked sad when she said, "Please, Dad can I take one of the puppies home with me?"

I got scared. What if she took me with her, away from my mother and the other dogs? The man she called "Dad," shook his head and said, "No, Kelly, we have to go home. Maybe we'll come back and play with the puppies some other time."

I was glad she wasn't taking me away, but I was also a little sad to see her go. I wondered if she really would come back.

I forgot about Kelly and Dad as the summer passed and the days got shorter and the leaves started turning red and gold. Michael took down the pen and built each of us a house. We spent much of our time tied to the poles just like the adult dogs, but Michael would still let us romp for a while every day.

He also started taking my brothers and sisters out for training runs. They were still too young to be on a team, but he was teaching them how to work as a team. He would put them into little houses built on the back of his pickup truck, then drive away, leaving me standing there all alone. He wouldn't give me a chance to be a sled dog.

One day when Michael returned from a training run, Kelly and Dad came back in their truck. Michael turned me and my brothers and sisters loose to play with Kelly. When she got tired and sat down to rest, I crawled onto her lap. I think that was my mistake.

She hugged me, and said to Dad, "Can I have this one?" What a dumb kid, I thought. I'm Michael's dog, he will never let me go with her.

Michael smiled at Kelly and said, "Okay, she's too small for my team anyway." He never took me with him, how did he know I was too small?

I jumped out of Kelly's lap and ran over to my
mother's house. Kelly came over and picked
me up and carried me over to Dad's truck. I
struggled and whimpered, looking back at my
mother and the other dogs. I knew I would
never see them again. I didn't even have time
to say goodbye.

CHAPTER 2

Their truck wasn't like Michael's. There was no dog box on the back. I sat in the front seat with them, instead of in the back, where sled dogs are supposed to be.

We drove for a long time. There weren't many trees in this new place, but there were lots of cars and houses. When we finally stopped, I was happy to get out of the truck and run around. I'd never sat still for that long before.

Other kids came over to Kelly's yard. I played with them all because I wasn't tied to a pole. They let me run all over the backyard because there was a fence around the yard. It was a tall, solid brown fence, and I couldn't see anything on the other side.

I was having fun with the kids, but I missed my mother and family. I wondered if they missed me, too. When Kelly brought me a dish of food, I got even lonelier thinking of the dinner Michael must have been cooking. But the food Kelly gave me was good. I thought, maybe this wouldn't be such a bad place to live after all.

When it started to get dark, they did a strange thing. They called me to come inside their house. I didn't know dogs could go into peoples' houses. Kelly let me explore the whole place; some of the floor was soft, and some was hard, shiny, and slippery. Once or twice, my feet slid out from under me. Kelly laughed each time.

There was another person in the house with Kelly and Dad; she was Kelly's mother. Kelly called her "Mom." When I saw Kelly with her mother, it really made me miss my mother even more. After a while, Mom and Dad told Kelly that it was time for bed.

Kelly took me into the living room where there was a big pillow on the floor. "Here's your bed, Judy," Kelly said, picking me up and putting me on the pillow. Everyone kissed me good night and turned off the lights. Some moonlight came in through the windows. This living room was a nice room, but it was too warm. I missed the cold, fresh scent of the outdoors. And the pillow was too soft. I longed for the scratchy straw in my dog house, and for the sounds of the dog lot.

For the first time, I missed the wind in the trees and the howls of the other dogs.

The next day was the same as the first. Lots of kids came over to play with Kelly and me. I ran with them around the yard, which was fun, but they always got tired before I did and I'd have to wait for them to stop panting. Even though I was running around, I felt frustrated that I had to stop at the fence. I felt penned-in, because I couldn't see what was on the other side of the fence.

Everyday was the same and I loved it. Then one day things changed. Instead of coming to breakfast in jeans, Kelly was wearing a dress. Dad had to tell her twice to hurry or she'd be late for school. When she was finished eating, she picked up a big bag and said, "Come on Judy, we're going to school."

She took me by the collar and led me out to the car, where Mom was waiting. We drove a short time, and stopped at the biggest building I'd ever seen. Kids were running and playing everywhere. This was going to be great, I thought. If some of the kids got tired playing with me, then others could take over. When Kelly opened the car door, I jumped over her legs and down to the ground.

"Judy come back here!" Kelly said, yelling at me. I'd never been talked to like that before, and the loud sound of her voice made me shrink down until my belly scraped the sidewalk. Kelly picked me up, looking a little sad. "Poor Judy, I'm not mad at you." She put me back on the seat. Mom said, "I wish Kelly were as eager to go to school as you are Judy." They both laughed and I felt better because they weren't mad at me. Then Kelly closed the car door and walked away with her friends.

As we drove back home, I wondered when Kelly would be home again. Mom played with me a little in the backyard, then said, "Judy, I have work to do in the house, you be a good dog and play out here."

When the back door shut, I felt really confused. What was I supposed to do out in the backyard all by myself? There was no one to play with and that stupid fence was keeping me from going anywhere. I wondered why Kelly wanted to take me away from my family, if she were going to leave me all alone.

It was the longest day I'd ever spent. Mom came outside a few times and played with me and gave me fresh water, but I was terribly lonely. I missed my family and my old home. The smell of my mother's coat was beginning to fade in my scent-memory.

When Kelly finally stepped through the door into the backyard, I was so happy to see her that I jumped straight into her arms. "Did you miss me while I was at school?" she asked. I licked her face to let her know that I sure did miss her!

We played in the backyard until Dad came home. Then we all went for a walk around the lake across the street. We sat down and watched the ducks swimming. Watching the mother and her babies made me miss my family again. Finally, Mom said, "It's time we go home." I was really excited and ran across the street to the truck. I thought we were going home to Michael's. But when they

caught up to me, Kelly took me by the collar and led me into the house. That's when it really hit me. This was my home, now. I wasn't going anywhere.

They talked all about me during dinner. I had already finished eating and was sitting by Kelly's chair, hoping she would give me some of what she was eating. It sure smelled good. They were saying "Judy" wasn't the right name for me. Since I looked like a fox, maybe I should be called, "Foxy."

I didn't like the name, Foxy. My name was Judy, that's what Michael called me. After everyone finished eating we went into the living room. Kelly held up one of my treats and said, "Come here, Foxy." I went over to her and she gave me the treat saying, "Good Foxy, good dog." Then Dad did the same thing. Then Mom did it too. I figured I could keep this up as long as the treats kept coming. They were so pleased with me, I decided to go along with them on this new name.

Goodbye Judy, I thought. Hello Foxy. It seemed the last link with my old home was

gone. But that night, I dreamed of my mother and the other dogs, and awoke with their ancestral howls in my ears. It took a long time for me to go back to sleep.

CHAPTER 3

School, I discovered, was a place where kids go because they have to. Kelly disappeared for days at a time, but would then be around all the time for two days in a row, wearing old clothes and playing and singing that she loved weekends. I didn't know what weekends were, but if they kept her home with me, then I loved them too.

We would go for walks around the lake almost every night. As the days got colder and colder, the last leaves fell off the trees and the ducks disappeared from the lake. One evening, instead of walking around the lake, they walked on the lake. How did they do that, I wondered? They had their whole bodies on top of the water. I ran down the hill, jumped on the water, and fell flat on my face. The water was hard and very slippery, so I got up slowly. "Poor Foxy," Kelly said, "she's never been on ice before."

This ice stuff was cold under my feet, but I didn't mind. Cold didn't bother me the way it seemed to bother parents. Kelly's parents were always telling her, "Put on your winter coat, it's cold outside." I wore my winter coat too. My black, white, and brown fur had grown thick and sleek as the weather changed from cool to cold.

One morning when Mom let me out, snow was falling. There was something about snow that I really liked. I think she knew, because she let me stay outside all day. I let the snow fall on me, then I shook it all off. I rolled on the now-white ground, and plowed my nose through the places were the snow was drifting.

I felt good, but I didn't know why. I remembered my mother would always tell us that sled dogs were different; the love of the outdoors was part of us.

That evening when Kelly brought me inside, I felt different. Usually after eating my supper, I would sit near Kelly while she ate her supper, hoping for a handout. That night I sat in front of the glass door, staring out into the yard. Although the moon was mostly covered by the clouds, the snowy yard seemed to glow with a bluish light. I felt drawn to it. I wanted to curl up in a bank of snow, to wrap myself in a blanket of Alaskan winter.

Dad noticed me. "The call of the wild," he said to Kelly, pointing at me.

I knew he was right. Somehow I seemed to hear wild howls in the chilly darkness of the city. It was only the wind, but something in me wanted to answer.

Snow fell almost every day after that. Sometimes it was only a few flakes; sometimes it fell all day long. Kelly would help Dad move the snow with a shovel, so the family would have a clear trail to walk. I never used the trail; it was more fun to jump and plow my way through the deep snow.

One night after supper, Dad brought out a new pink sled dog harness and put it on me. I was shocked; I didn't know city people had sled dog harnesses. At first the harness felt funny, like something that I would grow to fill.

We all went over to the lake. I ran and ran across the frozen lake. The more I ran the better the harness began to feel. I was feeling great. Then they tied Kelly's orange plastic toboggan to the harness.

I was disgusted. This wasn't the right kind of sled for a real sled dog. Dog sleds are made of light wood, with long runners holding a "basket" for riders or supplies. The musher drives by standing on the back of the runners. Not only were they not using the right kind of sled, but there weren't any other dogs. I wanted to be part of a team; I wasn't supposed to do all of the work.

As mad as I was, I also figured that if I did a good job, I might become a sled dog yet. So I took off running across the lake with the plastic toboggan tied behind me.

It was awful. The toboggan made a scraping, grating noise behind me on the snowy ice. When I slowed down, the toboggan kept going and banged into the back of my legs. So I ran faster and faster, trying to get away from the toboggan. I could hear them calling me to come back, but I just kept running across the lake. I ran up the bank on the other side of the lake and saw two kids playing with another plastic toboggan. I ran over to them. They untied the toboggan from the harness, and was I ever glad. Then they took me into a nearby house. They left me inside and went back outside.

Through the window I saw one of the kids using Kelly's toboggan. I got mad even though I didn't even like the thing. Then I noticed my family trudging up the bank of the lake, frozen air puffing from their mouths. Faintly I heard them calling my name. I barked and barked, but their ears must not have been as good as mine because they just walked away looking very sad.

How could they leave me? Then I thought, how could they find me? Would I have to stay here forever?

A long time later, a car pulled into the driveway. The two kids ran up to the car pointing to the house and to Kelly's toboggan. A man got out of the car, and came into the house.

He walked over to me and picked me up. Normally I don't like people doing that, but his face was kind and I was feeling lonesome. He felt my collar and looked at the green metal tag that Kelly had put there a long time ago. Then he said, "Well Foxy, let's get you home." I was so happy, I wiggled and barked and tried to kiss him. He laughed and carried me to his car.

We drove just a short distance and suddenly we were in front of my house. The man carried me to the door and rang the doorbell. When Kelly opened the door, he asked, "Did you lose a dog?" I barely heard him because Kelly was reaching for me. Kelly's parents came to the door, water was coming from everyone's eyes. I was so excited to be home, I went to the bathroom on Kelly's sweater. She didn't seem to mind.

I was home where I belonged. I was never going to leave again. Water was still coming from everyone's eyes when I laid down on my favorite spot on the rug. It felt great to be home. I slept well that night, and for many nights to come.

CHAPTER 4

One morning, Mom left me home when she took Kelly to school. Usually she would let me ride with her in the front seat. I wondered why she'd forgotten me.

I stared at the fence that kept me in the back yard. Then I ran toward it and found that fences were easy to jump. Running around to the front of the house, I took off in the direction of the school.

On our street, there were hardly any cars, but the closer I got to school, the louder and scarier the streets became. Cars and trucks were squealing and honking, coming at me from every direction. I was afraid when they got so close, but I was even more afraid to stop running.

When I saw the lady with the sign, I knew I was close to the school. Everyday I would see her from inside the car. She would walk into the middle of the street and hold up her sign to make the cars stop. Then the kids would walk across the street to the school. I ran as fast as I could, wondering when I would see

our car. The lady with the sign was waving her arms and hollering. Some kids turned and started yelling. They were all screaming and pointing at me.

One minute I was running; the next I was flying through the air. It happened so fast that my legs were still running even though I wasn't on the ground. Before I could understand any of it, the street was rushing back toward me.

I know I hit the ground hard, because I heard myself land. It sounded like the ice cracking on the lake; a dull, sickening THUD that sounds like danger, or death. But I didn't feel the landing. I couldn't feel anything. My mind was saying, "Move! Get Up! GO!" but nothing on my body would work.

A memory came to me then, of being tiny and helpless, newborn and blind. Shortly after I was born, I was taken away from my mother. It was just for a short period of time, but I remembered shivering and twitching, poking my sightless head this way and that in search of warmth and comfort. When I was put back with my mother, she bathed me tenderly and

settled me into the straw bed close to her heart.

Lying on the sidewalk, I felt that same sense of helplessness. This time, no one comforted me.

The screams I'd heard got closer, along with the sounds of running feet. A man was bending over me, trying to pick me up. Pain jolted one of my back legs and flooded through my body like boiling water, scalding where numbness had been. I tried to bite him, to make him put me down, but my mouth wouldn't work. Then the lights went out.

When the lights came back on, I was lying on the front seat of our car. Mom was driving and every jolt of the car made the hurt boil faster. I saw the pain the way I could see the cooking fire in Michael's back yard. The flames would heat the metal pot until it glowed, making what was inside bubble.

Water was coming from Mom's eyes as she said over and over again, "Oh Foxy, don't worry, you'll be fine."

She stopped the car and carried me into a place I remembered. We had come here for my shots, which I hated. The memory exhausted me. I was already hurting enough.

The lights went out again. When they came back on, I was lying on a table. Dad was there and so was my doctor. She was touching my painful bones. She told them that I had a broken hip and even if she did operate, I might never walk again. My doctor suggested the best thing to do was to put me to sleep. I was scared and confused. Why wouldn't I be able to walk again? And I'd already had enough sleep.

Mom must have known that, because she said she didn't want me to be put to sleep. She told the doctor to operate. "All right," the doctor said. "Just don't expect Foxy to be able to walk very well, or at all."

Walk very well? I thought. I'm a sled dog. I don't walk. I run.

The doctor didn't tell the truth, because as soon as they left the room, the first thing she did was put something on my face until I went to sleep.

When I opened my eyes again, I knew things were different. Part of me was very cold. I saw that some of the fur on my leg and back was gone. A red line with black dots cut through the bare spot, and it hurt very badly. I wanted to tear that line out of my body. But my head was tied down, and I couldn't reach the sore spot.

Soon the doctor came back and looked closely at my leg. She nodded to herself but didn't touch me. I jerked my head hard against the restraints, trying to show her where it hurt. She spoke to me in a gentle voice. "I know it hurts, Foxy, but you must lie still and let those stitches heal."

When she left the room, I wondered if I would always hurt this badly.

CHAPTER 5

The pain was bad that day and the next. The doctor tried to get me to eat, but I couldn't eat any food. She even tried to give me my favorite treat, raw liver, but I didn't want it. I lay very still, trying not to hurt my sore spots.

When Kelly and her parents came to take me home, I was so happy I forgot about how badly I felt. Even though it hurt to ride home in the car, I didn't care. I just snuggled down in Kelly's lap and rested my head on her arm. Usually when I'm happy, I wiggle all over; this time, I was too sore. But I think Kelly knew how happy I felt; her smile showed me how much she loved me and was happy to have me with her again.

My bed had extra pillows on it, and it felt soft and comforting to my aching body. There was even a pillow for my head. I lay there for many days unable to walk. Everyone had to take turns carrying me outside to go to the bathroom. How embarrassing for a sled dog to have to be carried outside to go to the bathroom. I was really glad when eventually I could hobble outside by myself.

Gradually, it got easier to walk. Kelly would take me for walks around the lake as I grew stronger. Sometimes she would try to get me to run. I really didn't want to, because I knew it would hurt and it scared me to think about running. I remembered the accident, when the running turned into flying and the flying turned into terrible pain. Such speed could be deadly.

The thought of running made me shiver. I could be coaxed into trotting, but nothing faster. It bothered Kelly, but I couldn't help it. I could only hope she wasn't too disappointed with me.

Then one night I dreamed of my mother. She was skimming across a snowy landscape that gleamed in the moonlight. Unfettered by harness, the icy wind flowing through her thick, dark coat, she seemed to float above the snowy trail.

"We run," she called out to me. "That's what sled dogs do. We run."

Before I woke up completely, I felt my legs twitching in a kind of dream-running. Asleep,

I had been trying to keep up with my mother. Awake, I knew I had to overcome my fears, because sled dogs run.

I tried to run that day when Kelly took me for my walk. The pain was there but it slowly faded the more I ran. Soon I was running very fast again. I could feel strength slowly creeping back into my body and endurance fleshing out my thin legs.

I especially liked running on the sandy beach when we would go on a fishing trip. While her parents fished, Kelly and I would run down long stretches of sand that felt soft and giving under my feet. Kelly would always get tired long before I did. Sometimes I got so thrilled by my own speed that I'd leave her far behind, running until I could barely hear her shouting my name. Then I'd sneak back feeling guilty, my tail tucked between my legs. Kelly would look angry until she saw me creeping back toward her, my belly scraping the sand. By then she would have caught her breath, and she'd always laugh and pet me. My tail would spring back and wave.

Those fishing trips were great. They would bring back salmon; fillets for them and everything else for me. My dinners started smelling more like the ones Michael used to fix. Sometimes I wondered about the dog lot. Were my brothers and sisters on Michael's team? Were they real sled dogs now? Did the wind still howl around the mountains? Were the trees shedding their leaves like the ones in my yard?

I brooded about such things as the rain fell. Day after day it rained, sometimes lightly, sometimes like a battering drum on the roof. We rarely saw the sun. I hated rain. I wanted snow.

When the first snow finally fell that autumn, I was so happy I ran around the yard all by myself. Kelly had to drag me indoors for the night. This was camping-out weather as far as I was concerned.

One night Dad came home with a huge smile on his face. He told Kelly he had a surprise for her. Kelly stopped doing her homework and we all went outside. In the back of his truck was a dog sled. A real dog sled! It was just like the one Michael had, only a little smaller.

"Tomorrow night we'll take Foxy out on the lake and see if she's strong enough to pull it," he told Kelly. "Tonight, I'll show you how to use it."

How dumb, I thought. I'm the one who will use it; all Kelly has to do is stand on the back. How difficult could that be? He took the sled into the garage, and after dinner he and Kelly spent a long time in there, talking about how to drive the sled and how to stay on the runners. I sulked in the kitchen. I wanted to try it right away. I couldn't wait another whole day.

The next day crawled by until Kelly came home from school. Dad took so long getting home I was afraid the snow would melt before he arrived. Then they had to eat dinner and clean the dishes. My own dinner was untouched; my stomach was too tight to put food into it.

We all walked to the lake, Kelly carrying my harness and Dad pulling the sled. The harness was the same pink one we'd used before. This time the harness fit much better, like a part of me that had been missing until now. When I was hooked to the sled, Dad told Kelly to stand on the brake. He then walked out to the middle of the lake, and yelled, "Okay, let her go!"

Kelly released the brake and yelled, "Go, Foxy, Go!" I felt a thrill that left me light-headed. It was my chance to run.

And run I did, straight toward Dad who yelled, "Come here, Foxy! Come here!" Behind me Kelly was screaming, "Run Foxy! Run!" I felt perfectly balanced between the earth and the sky. My feet were on the ground, but I was flying.

Dad had to grab the sled to make me stop. He and Kelly laughed at the way my tongue hung down as I gulped for air. "Can we do it again Dad," Kelly asked. You bet we can, I thought.

We ran several more times that night; Kelly complained when Dad told her we had to go

home. Every night after that, the three of us were out on the lake. Sometimes I did speed work: straightaway, dead runs across the lake toward Dad with his stopwatch. Other nights, I circled the lake, running around and around its snowy perimeter to build strength and endurance. Kelly was learning to help me by "kicking," shoving one foot against the snow to give added push to my pull.

Kelly heard the kids at school talking about junior sled dog races which were about to start in town. One night during dinner she asked her parents if she and I could race in the one-dog class. I remembered the racing champions my mother had told me about. I realized I could never race that fast, but the idea of a race really excited me. Even if I didn't win, I'd be part of their tradition — a very small part, but still a part.

Kelly's parents told her we would have to work hard if we wanted to be competitive in the races. From that moment on, the stopwatch became my enemy. Little by little we trimmed our time down, cutting second after second until the seconds turned into minutes. If we were going to race, I was going to be ready.

My legs tightened with muscle. I became leaner each day, despite the huge dinners I bolted down each evening.

Sometimes my training went further than my strength. I'd collapse into my bed and stare at the wall, my legs burning and trembling with exhaustion. But the pain was nothing like the pain of the accident, and I knew it would be gone by morning. As my training continued, gradually the burning and trembling in my legs disappeared.

I knew I was in great physical shape. I was impatient to run. Bring on the races, I kept thinking. It's time, it's my time to run.

CHAPTER 6

My training continued for a few more days. Then one night there was no more training. Dad told Kelly that we weren't going to train, because the race was the next day. He wanted us to relax and go to bed early. "Tomorrow we will have to get up early and go to the race," he said.

I laid awake for a long time, wondering what the race was going to be like. I knew my mother would have been proud of me. I didn't dream of her that night. I had no dreams at all.

The next morning we rode in the truck to the race track. There were lots of trucks like Michael's with little compartments in the back. I was sitting in the front seat, as usual. When the other dogs poked their heads out of their little compartments, I was embarrassed to be seen in the front seat.

All sizes of kids were there. Some were old enough to harness their own two, three, or five-dog teams. Others were very small; they stood bundled in snowsuits and scarves, looking apprehensive as their parents harnessed their dogs. Kelly hooked me up to her sled and Dad helped us get to the starting line. There were two other one-dog teams ahead of us.

I heard a voice high in the air, and looked up. Kelly did too. Dad told her that the people in the tall building kept time with their stopwatches. Then I heard the voice again: "FIVE—FOUR—THREE—TWO— ONE—GO!" The first team took off down the trail and disappeared into the trees. Everyone was yelling, even Kelly. I wanted to win this race, to prove that I was a real sled dog.

Soon we saw the team coming back out of the trees, toward a group of people on the other side of the tall building. "That's the finish line over there," Dad told Kelly.

I looked at the trail, then at the finish line. I was supposed to take off down the trail in front of us, go through the woods and end up on the trail by the finish line. I wondered if there were a short cut.

The next team was ready to race. When the voice said "GO!" they took off just like the

first team. Kelly was fidgeting a little; I could feel nervous, squirmy vibrations coming from the sled through my harness. Then after the second team crossed the finish line, I heard "GO!" and felt Kelly release the brake. I leaped, and the harness responded. We were gliding down the hard-packed trail, the shouts of the people watching echoing in our ears.

The trail we were on went in a big loop back to the finish line. Why go all the way down to the trees, I thought, when I could just cut across the middle to the other side of this loop? So I turned and headed for the trail to the finish line.

What a mistake. The snow was much deeper in the middle, and not packed down at all. I floundered and dragged my way through, the sled pitching so wildly that Kelly fell off. Somehow I scrambled out of the deep snow and ran driver-less to the finish line.

The people weren't cheering any more, they were laughing. The voice in the tall building said that Kelly and Foxy were disqualified. I wondered if that meant we won the race. The look on the Dad's face told me we didn't win. Kelly had the same look when she stumbled over the finish line, snow-covered and panting.

No one talked on the way home. They were upset and I was responsible. I wanted to win so much. I wondered if I would get another chance to do it right and prove that I was a sled dog, a good sled dog.

That night at dinner, Kelly asked if we could practice at the track before the next race. Her parents thought it was a good idea. That meant I would get another chance. Kelly was excited to practice at the track, but I could still tell she was mad at me for dumping her off the sled into the deep snow.

The next afternoon, the whole family went back to the track. No one else was there. Dad harnessed me at the starting line and told Kelly to step on the brake. Mom went over to the finish line, then Dad ran down the trail toward the trees.

I wanted to run after him but Kelly was still standing on the brake. I looked back at her;

she was putting on a fur hat with ear flaps because it was a bitter cold day. Before her face disappeared in the hat, I caught a glimpse of her expression; she was still mad at me. This made me even more determined to do it right this time. No short cuts.

When I heard Dad yell, "GO!" I waited a second or two after Kelly stepped off the brake. I wanted to make sure she was ready. Then I took off down the trail that already seemed familiar to me.

The snow was crisp and packed under my feet. It sparkled brilliantly under the winter sun, which was already dipping low in the sky. In the distance, the snowdrifts looked almost purple. I was running for fun, savoring the feel of the trail. Dad must have known, because he started yelling, "Come on, Foxy! You can do better than that!" Then he turned and ran down the trail.

It was a challenge I couldn't refuse. The sled runners began hissing with speed. Kelly was shouting, "Go, Foxy, go!" She didn't sound mad at me any more. I caught Dad and passed him like he was standing still. I heard him laugh as the sled whipped past.

The run was ending much too soon. I could see Mom at the finish line and she grabbed at the sled as we went past. Kelly used the brake to bring us to a stop. It felt like we had just started when we were finished. Mom gave me a piece of raw liver, my favorite treat. Kelly pulled off her hat, uncovering a huge smile on a face so flushed with excitement that I couldn't see her freckles any more. She gave me a big hug and told me what a good sled dog I was. She didn't even complain about my liver breath when I gave her a big kiss. Dad soon joined us. He was panting and out of breath, but his smile was even bigger than Kelly's.

"I think we've got ourselves a sled dog," he said. As he unharnessed me, he told Kelly we'd run here every afternoon so I'd know what to do in the next race. I already knew what to do, but I figured I'd go along with the plan. It seemed to make him happy to think he was teaching me something.

W e ran every afternoon, just as he had promised. Every time he yelled, "GO!" I was determined to make the run better and faster than the last. Kelly worked with me, kicking as hard as she could and singing at the top of her lungs. I particularly liked the song about the star-spangled banner — the high notes were almost as good as the howling of the dogs in Michael's lot. Funny, I hardly thought much about my old home anymore, although I still dreamed about my mother from time to time.

One afternoon it started snowing as Dad harnessed me. He looked worried. "Hope this doesn't last," he said. "We don't want the trail to be covered with fresh snow for tomorrow's race. We need it packed hard to take advantage of Foxy's speed."

I loved the fresh snow, and hoped that it would last. It felt like winter was tickling me as I romped through the swirling flakes. It made me so playful that I didn't want the run to be over. I rolled all over the ground after I was unharnessed, and grabbed Kelly's fur hat from her hand, daring her to chase me for it. Dad smiled at me, but frowned at the thick clouds that unfolded sheets of snow and hid the early sunset.

It was still snowing the next morning when we arrived at the track for the second race of the season. The track wasn't quite as crowded as it had been for the first race. Kelly and I were going to be the second team to race. When the voice in the tall building told the first team to go, the start wasn't very fast. The dog was really big, but was struggling through the deep snow that covered the once-packed trail. Snow was falling so heavily that I could hardly see the trees where we turn. It took a very long time for the first team to cross the finish line, and the dog looked exhausted.

When I heard our signal to go, a funny thing happened; I was running as fast as I could but not moving very quickly. The snow was grabbing at my legs, and the sled felt so heavy I wondered if Dad were on there instead of Kelly.

I bent my head and dug my feet into the grasping drifts. We floundered along, the runners squeaking reluctantly through the wet, heavy snow. Somewhere up ahead I heard Mom and Dad calling my name, but I couldn't see them. Kelly shouted encouragement from behind; her words pushed me forward. When we finally crossed the finish line, I fell into Mom's arms. She carried me to the truck and gave me some liver. I could hardly chew my favorite food in the whole world. A little while later, Kelly came running up to me and gave me a big hug. She was holding a red ribbon. We had come in second place, my legs felt like we had come in 100th. I was happy to win a ribbon, but I was more happy to rest my head in Kelly's lap while we drove home.

As I laid there, I remembered my mother's stories about the Iditarod, the 1,000 mile sled dog race from Anchorage to Nome; of the deep snow, the dreadful winds, and the numbing cold. How could those dogs run 1,000 miles, I wondered? It was all I could do to finish a one-dog race.

I rested for a few days, then it was back to the track again to practice for the next race. I was delighted to see that the snow was once again packed hard and flat. Kelly told her Dad that they had done a good job grooming the trail.

I ran as fast as I could during our practice runs, with Kelly singing behind me and Dad smiling at the finish line. There were lots of mushers practicing on those short bright winter afternoons. Some were grownups with teams of ten and more dogs, but there were lots of kids, too. I figured we'd have plenty of competition at the next race.

We did. The parking lot was packed with dog trucks and filled with the voices of excited dogs. It was a sunny day with temperatures that made the snow crispy underpaw and reddened kids' faces. Parents were wrapping their children in hats and scarves, since their skin couldn't take the cold air and the speed of a moving sled. They used the words "wind-chill factor" a lot on days like this.

There were plenty of kids competing in the one-dog class. Kelly counted 12 teams. We would be going out number eight. I could tell Kelly didn't want to wait for 7 other teams to finish before we started. I jumped around nervously. It seemed to take forever before it was our turn at the starting line. Watching the other 7 teams take off, I could tell the trail was going to be very fast.

The memory of that race will stay with me forever. The sled seemed to float behind me, hovering like the vapor that puffed from my wide-open mouth. Bits of snow flew up as my feet pounded the trail. I could feel Kelly kicking regularly, stroking speed from the snow. We were a team, and I loved it.

I was running fast but, I was holding back my best. I had learned to save a little bit of energy for the end. As we neared the finish line, I released my complete power, bending

my head and letting my legs spring loose with a fluid shiver. I no longer thought about winning; I simply ran. Blood was pounding in my ears, sounding a two-word drumbeat -- we run, we run, we run. It was the sound of my mother's legacy.

The people at the finish were just a blur as we skidded past. Even though Kelly was standing on the brake she had difficultly stopping the sled. Finally, someone grabbed the sled and we stopped. Everyone was shaking Kelly's hand and patting her on the back. I just stood where I was, my legs quivering as they accustomed themselves to the stillness once more. I didn't know how we did, but I could tell we did very well.

I didn't need anyone to carry me to the truck that day. When Kelly unhooked my harness from the sled, I ran to the truck and jumped into the front seat. I wasn't embarrassed to sit there anymore. I was proud to sit up front and ride with my family.

Kelly gave me a liver treat and she sipped on some hot chocolate while we waited for the other mushers to finish. I was very pleased

with my performance, but I was still
surprised when I heard the voice high in the
air say, "The winner of the one-dog class
today is Kelly and her dog Foxy!"

Kelly ran to the finish line, and came dancing
back to the truck with a blue ribbon in her
hand. She hugged me and whispered in my
ear, "We did it Foxy, you are the best sled dog
in the whole world." I gave her a big liver-

breath kiss. I was so happy. Only one thing would have made me happier. I wished my mother and Michael would have been able to see me race.

Kelly hung up our blue ribbon on the fireplace mantel, right by my favorite spot. I looked at the ribbon a lot, thinking that things couldn't get any better. But I was wrong; we won the next two races. Two more blue ribbons joined my first one, and then, because we had won three of the five races, Kelly was given a trophy with a little dog on the top. She was very proud of the trophy and kept it in her room, but I didn't care. I had my three blue ribbons.

At dinner one night, Dad told Kelly there was going to be one more race. Because we won the one-dog class, we were eligible to compete in the Junior World Championship Sled Dog Race which was going to be held in a few weeks. The best teams from all over the State of Alaska and Canada would be competing in this special race.

Kelly told Dad that we would have to practice hard if we were to win. He told her not to get her hopes up, because the Junior World Championship Race would be a much different race with a lot of very, very, good sled dogs. Kelly reminded him that she had the best sled dog in the world. He patted her on the head and said, "We'll see in two weeks."

CHAPTER 8

The Junior World Championship Sled Dog Race was, in-deed, a much different race. We had to race three days in a row. The total time after three days of racing would determine the winner, the Junior World Champion.

Our practicing continued every night. One night, Dad showed Kelly how to put wax on the runners so the sled would go faster. I thought that was ridiculous. I did the pulling and Kelly did the kicking; we made the sled go fast, not something on the runners.

The night before the first day of the race, I dreamed not of my mother, but of a dozen other dogs. They were of different sizes and colors, but they ran as a perfectly matched team, their rhythm joyous. I realized I was a part of the team, harnessed among the other dogs, surrounded by their exhilaration. I was one of them. We could run forever.

We didn't. I was still asleep when Kelly came down stairs and started making her breakfast. She was too excited to do more than pick at her food, and I was too nervous to beg for leftovers.

The race track was jammed with trucks and people. Sleds were being unloaded and strings of dogs were tied everywhere. All of the dogs were bigger than me and looked fast and formidable. I tried not to let that worry me.

Kelly and I were so excited, it was very hard for us to wait for our turn. I went to the bathroom four times before we went to the starting line. Kelly went twice.

I decided not to let those big, out-of-town dogs bother me. This was my track; I had raced and won here. I kept telling myself this race would be just like the others, except we'd have to do it three times.

Maybe it was the excitement of all the people watching, or maybe it was the challenge of all those other dogs, but as soon as we left the starting line, I realized this race would be different. The trail was hard and fast; I could scarcely feel the sled behind me. Once, I even looked back to see if Kelly had forgotten to get on the runners. It was almost as if I were surrounded by the dogs from my dream. I was using their imagined strength and blending it with my own. I soared down the track

without even thinking of the other teams we had to beat.

When our run was complete, a few people took my picture. I was so hot that I ate some snow while I waited for my liver and water. Kelly was pacing back and forth waiting for all of the teams to finish. Then we heard the voice high in the air say, "Here are the times and places for the first day of racing in the one-dog class. In first place, with a time of I minute and 21 seconds is Kelly...." We never heard the rest because everyone was yelling and jumping up and down. It didn't matter to me what else the voice said. I had heard what I needed to hear. We were in first place. Now we just had to stay there.

The second day of racing was almost like the first. Kelly and I worked so hard we almost melted the trail. That day, I wasn't so nervous. I was able to look at the other dogs without feeling small. I'd finally figured out that being small wasn't something to be ashamed of, it was just the way I was.

After the second day, we were still in first place but only by 5 seconds. If I could work just as hard the last day, as I did the first two, we could be the Junior World Champions of the one-Dog Class.

I was eager for sleep that night, hoping that once again I would become part of that wild, imaginary team and draw strength from it. But I had no dreams that night; it was a night of thick darkness. I woke up feeling rested, yet somehow depleted. Could I really win? Did I have what it takes to be a great sled dog? Could I follow in my mother's pawsteps?

Once we arrived at the track, I felt like the spark was gone. I knew I had the ability, but I wasn't sure if I could command it. Panicky, I tried to block out the noise, the crowd, the sights and scents of the other dogs at the track. The only thing I could think about was how proud my mother and Michael would have been if they could have seen me.

Because we had the fastest time we were the first team to race. As we were waiting at the starting line for the high voice to say, "GO!," I looked over at Dad one last time before we started to race. I couldn't believe what I saw, Dad was talking to Michael! I shook myself

all over as if to shake off new fallen snow that wasn't falling. Michael had come to see me race. I said to myself, "All right Michael, you've come to see a sled dog race, just watch me!"

I was thinking too much. Every step was for Michael. I wanted to show him that I had become a good sled dog after all. I was so busy thinking about Michael, that I almost forgot to turn on the trail through the trees. Kelly yelled at me just in time, or I would have missed the turn.

I was afraid I'd wasted precious seconds, but when we crossed the finish line everyone was cheering and screaming. I walked proudly to the truck to get my treat and wait for the other teams to finish. Michael patted me on the head and said, "Judy you are a great sled dog. I wish you were on my team." Dad must not have told him about my new name, but it didn't matter what he called me, I knew he still loved me, but I was Kelly's team now. I was part of her family. I knew he understood.

It seemed to take forever for the other teams to finish, then we heard what we were waiting to hear. The high voice boomed, "The winner of the Junior One-Dog World Championship Sled Dog Race is Kelly and her dog Foxy!"

My legs felt like we had just won the Iditarod. I had to sit down in the middle of the cheering people who were hugging Kelly and taking endless pictures of all of us.

We had a big celebration that night. I was even able to have a piece of cake without having to beg some from Kelly. Everyone was having a good time until Dad told Kelly that if she wanted to race next year, she would have to race in the two-dog class. He said, "We'll have to get another dog to race with Foxy."

My cake didn't taste that good anymore. Why did we need another dog? I was a world champion. I didn't want to share my family, to share my yard, or to teach another dog to race.

For the next few days, all Kelly talked about was the new dog. I wasn't sure if I ever wanted to race again. I didn't want to teach some rookie how to race. This new dog would probably just slow me down or embarrass me.

The day finally came: Kelly and Dad left in the truck to get the new dog. They didn't take me along, and I was glad. I sulked around the house until I heard the truck pull into the driveway. Mom took me out to the front porch to meet this new dog.

The first thing I saw was this new dog sitting in my spot in the front seat of the truck. That made me mad. I thought, this dog has a lot to learn. The front seat is mine.

There was something familiar about the dog, but the glare on the windshield made it difficult to see the dog clearly. When they let the dog out of the truck, I took a good, long, angry look. Then I froze.

This new dog was Rosie, my mother!

I jumped in the air, like the people at the race. I ran to her and kissed her all over. She

kissed me and we rolled in the snow like puppies.

I couldn't wait for the races next year. I would be running with one of the best sled dogs in the world. Her years on the trail could teach me so much. Maybe we would win the Junior World Championship Two-Dog Class.

But more importantly for now, I hoped there would be room for both of us in the front seat of our truck.